T0171720

THE GREATEST STRATEGIST

KALEB KOHLHASE

WESTBOW
PRESS®
A DIVISION OF THOMAS NELSON
& ZONDERVAN

WestBow Press books may be ordered through booksellers or by contacting:

WestBow Press
A Division of Thomas Nelson & Zondervan
1663 Liberty Drive
Bloomington, IN 47403
www.westbowpress.com
844-714-3454

Scripture quotations are taken from the Holy Bible, New Living Translation, copyright © 1996, 2004, 2015 by Tyndale House Foundation. Used by permission of Tyndale House Publishers, Inc., Carol Stream, Illinois 60188. All rights reserved.

ISBN: 979-8-3850-0085-2 (sc)
ISBN: 979-8-3850-0086-9 (e)

Library of Congress Control Number: 2023911057

Print information available on the last page.

WestBow Press rev. date: 06/15/2023

CONTENTS

INTRODUCTION

I heard arguments from some of my friends during college. I've seen comments on the internet. I've listened to a lot of criticism from acquaintances about the Bible. I've even wrestled with some of the mentioned questions myself. Specifically speaking, these comments usually refer to very particular verses or concepts that require a little more thought. I want to establish a point of view that provides greater context to the overall tone of some scripture and brings to light an idea that gives a greater understanding of the metanarratives of scripture.

Christians like me hold these beliefs: God is the King of all Kings, the Lord of all Lords, and Priest of all Priests; He is exalted above all. If God is the greatest King, He is the best at what a king should do. One underlying narrative of all scripture is a great spiritual war between good and evil. The end described in the book of Revelation is a war to end all wars. There will be warfare between the Prince of Evil and the King of Light. We ought to keep this in our minds, but there are current battles we should focus on now. Warfare requires a great deal of strategy, so I'd like to show that God is the Greatest Strategist because He is the King above all Kings.

The first thing I'd like to do is establish cultural background by discussing the three ancient languages of the Bible. The brief review of language may show why some scripture sounds in a way some may call "harsh" and why it might sometimes seem contradictory.

1

LANGUAGES OF
THE BIBLE

The Bible was originally written in three ancient languages. Two (Hebrew and Aramaic) are specific to the current area known as the Middle East. The other language, Greek, is well known today. A book called *Evidence That Demands a Verdict* by Josh and Sean McDowell has some good insight I'll refer to for help. Sean and Josh quote Larry Walker from his book, *The Origin of the Bible*. Larry, a former professor of Old Testament and Semitic Languages at Mid-America Baptist Theological Seminary, says, "Hebrew, like the other early Semitic languages, concentrates on observation more than reflection" (Walker 2012, 218–221). Then, a little farther in the next paragraph, Walker describes Aramaic. "Aramaic is linguistically very close to Hebrew and similar in structure. In contrast to Hebrew, Aramaic uses a larger vocabulary, including many loan words, and greater variety of connectives" (Walker 2012, 228–230). When I read those descriptions of the original languages of the Old Testament, they helped me understand why the English version sounds so direct. The third language, Ancient Greek, was used to retranslate the Old Testament (also known as the Septuagint). This was the same language primarily spoken around the time of the New Testament era. Again, *Evidence That Demands a Verdict* quotes Walker describing the language as "beautiful, rich, and harmonious as an instrument of communication. Ancient Greek was a 'language of argument'" (Walker 2012, 230–234).

When we read the Old Testament, it is essential to remember that the language was remarkably concise. The original authors sometimes provided only finer details about certain verses. Some verses can sound quite harsh to the point that they may seem to contradict what we know about God in the New Testament. Forgetting details, such as depth of language, leads to confusion. The context of surrounding verses and chapters matters, so we should always try to be aware of previous events. Since the book is incredibly detailed and lengthy, I find it necessary to carefully read and take notes, lest I forget important verses.

Some historical practices come into play that aren't necessarily described in scripture but are pertinent. The lack of those details doesn't mean there is an error; rather, the original authors didn't think it was necessary to mention those details because they weren't writing for future generations thousands of years later. Instead, they were recording events for their current generation. It is critical to know we are reading from a point of view that addresses people of that age. This also doesn't mean there is no current meaning in the text. This is one of the great mysteries of scripture; it is applicable to everyone yet was written for specific historical groups. We should consider the author's point of view and remember the intended audience to understand the Old Testament properly. The same is true for the New Testament; however, those books are much more modern because the language is newer.

QUESTION 1: THERE ARE CONTRADICTIONS IN THE BIBLE. HOW CAN IT BE LEGITIMATE?

Translation differences and missing details from context can lead to misunderstandings of various historical texts. Let's look at a few examples brought up by many where words might seem to contradict common knowledge. Whenever I refer to verses, I always use the New Living Translation, since I find it easiest to understand while preserving the original context. Longer selections of verses can be found in the verse appendix except when I refer to chapters for the sake of brevity. Exodus 20:5 says, "You must not bow down to them or worship them, for I, the Lord your God, am a jealous God who will not tolerate your affection for any other gods. I lay the sins of the parents upon their children; the entire family is affected—even children in the third and fourth generations of those who reject me." At first, readers may think, *Hey, doesn't the Bible say we shouldn't be jealous?* or *Isn't jealousy a sin?* Those statements are true, and accountability is important. As Christians, we believe God cannot sin. However, it would help if we investigated a particular linguistic nuance here. The Greek and Hebrew translations have different meanings for the word *jealousy* in this verse. The word here isn't referring to the same jealousy filled with envy and greed people have. Rather, this jealousy is more of a zealous, loving desire; God is begging reverence for Himself. The authors of many English translations use the closest word equivalent in this case. English words can have more than one meaning and may lack the details of the original word. Since most of us don't speak those ancient languages anymore, nuance can be easily forgotten.

Another example is found in Judges 9:56: "In this way, God punished Abimelech for the evil he had done against his father by murdering his seventy brothers." The New Living Translation uses the word *murder*, but the English Standard Version uses *kill*. Either would be technically appropriate because *murder* can also mean "kill." Since God planned it to be that way, the technical definition of *murder* through premeditation is most likely why some translations use that word. However, this doesn't mean God is doing murder unlawfully, because the consequence meets the behavior in His eyes. God established the law, and Abimelech's sons suffered the ultimate consequence of sin: death.

As the last example, there is a question asked in confusion about Cain that relates to the question above. I have heard, "How did Cain marry when nobody except Abel, Adam, and Eve existed at the time? Doesn't this imply incest?" This presupposition comes from Genesis 4:17: "Cain had sexual relations with his wife, and she became pregnant and gave birth to Enoch. Then Cain founded a city, which he named Enoch after his son." There is no evidence before this verse suggesting Adam and Eve had more children. I have concluded that the story doesn't always follow chronological order as recorded. I realized this because the next chapter discusses Adam's lineage from his third son, Seth. The Bible says only that Adam had other sons and daughters besides Seth without naming each one. Each documented descendant also had unnamed sons and daughters.

Let me pose a counterquestion to emphasize my point. When do sexual relations quit being immediate and immoral? We marry either men or women today, and biblical records show we all have ancestors tied back to Adam and Eve. Yet we don't call our wives or husbands true brothers and sisters by blood. Genesis 5 shows that there were many unnamed relatives. Eventually, cousins of cousins and of cousins would have to have married, given that was the only way to procreate.

Surprisingly, this practice is still acceptable today. There is enough genetic difference between second cousins and beyond (there are rare occasions in some states where a DNA test can be ordered for first cousins). Thus, logically, Cain must have married one of his descendants.

QUESTION 2: THERE ARE MANY INTERPRETATIONS OF SCRIPTURE. HOW CAN WE KNOW FOR SURE WHAT IT SAYS?

One particularly tricky thing about writing is the "personal take." Books are open to personal understanding. The Holy Scriptures by that logic can be seen in different ways. There is some truth in that simply because we aren't God. We don't always fully understand the depth of His Word. Scripture plainly uses language that shows us to be fools compared to Him. See Proverbs 3:5; Romans 12:2; James 3:12–18; 1 Corinthians 3:18; and Proverbs 3:7. From this selection, we see that true godly wisdom doesn't boast. Humility must be practiced in the process. We should admit when we don't understand something.

Scripture also tells us we need to meditate on it; see Joshua 1:8. We must reflect on His words. Bible study shouldn't be a casual exercise either. There needs to be careful and deep thought. Some verses have a plain meaning. Others can be quite perplexing. I think the best way to make sense of difficulties is to have a support system. First, pray that God might give you His wisdom. Remember to always start with Him. Reflect on difficult and easy verses to see what you get out of them first. Then, if you are struggling, ask a friend. Keep on asking more knowledgeable people. Also, remember to continue praying through the process of asking people. The Holy Spirit will help you when you are seeking Him. For example, I often refer to the Got Questions website when I encounter difficult biblical questions. I also ask friends or church elders who know more about scripture than I do. When everything you try fails to answer your question adequately, pray to God and admit you can't grasp it. You don't have to have an answer that makes sense or makes you feel good. The most crucial part is that you've tried and depended on God throughout the process. You might say, "How did I depend on God if I asked other people?" God works through people *and* His Spirit. Sure, people don't have full authority over what the Word says. However, at the same time, God entrusts people to teach it. God has the final authority. We ought to seek His wisdom. "Leaning not on your own understanding" is also a call to be humble.

Even what I write now is subject to interpretation. I hope there is true wisdom in what I say, but I need better understanding too. I have asked many, if not all, the same questions in this book. My mind is susceptible to doubt, criticism, and skepticism. The Lord has been overwhelmingly patient with me. Surprisingly, being at war in your mind may be a good sign. Does the devil need to attack those with no defense after all? When you seek out people, be cautious. Wolves in sheep's clothing are tricky to spot. God will give discernment when asked. In some ways, God placed multiple meanings in some verses so we can ponder His mysterious ways. There must be caution about finding meaning that wasn't meant to be there. The ultimate guide to finding more meaning is to base your thought on other pieces of scripture. The Word of God can back the Word of God, but our interpretation may lead to corruption. We have to test everything utilizing other scripture.

QUESTION 3: HOW CAN SO MANY TRANSLATIONS BE TRUSTED?

It's important to know that some English translations stick to the literal Greek transcript rather than rewording text to make it easier to understand. Having various English versions doesn't necessarily mean validity and verifiability are reduced. It is essential to be critical of things that are reworded, of course. Translations need to have the same spirit or relative meaning to hold validity. Generally speaking, it is a good idea to compare multiple versions to see if certain words are missing or changed that provide critical context. I don't know whether I completely understand why different groups thought there needed to be different ways of saying the same things in this instance. On one hand, having different perspectives with choices in language can help people understand something better. On the other, this can sow distrust in skeptical people. Some translations may have risen from divisions in the church. The disciples never intended this; see 1 Corinthians 1:10: "I appeal to you, dear brothers and sisters, by the authority of our Lord Jesus Christ, to live in harmony with each other. Let there be no divisions in the church. Rather, be of one mind, united in thought and purpose." I can see why various English translations sow this kind of distrust in scripture. Many say that all these versions show people can simply change what is recorded.

On the contrary, let me establish a point of view that might help. There is another side to the whole concept of an English version of the Bible: the process of physical translation to English itself. I mentioned the Septuagint earlier; this is a careful word-for-word translation of ancient Hebrew and Aramaic to ancient Greek. This included the Old Testament and then what the apostles or disciples wrote. Creating an English translation is incredibly difficult because of the differences between these three languages. Several groups of expert biblical scholars have looked into the Septuagint text in great depth. They have the exceptionally difficult job of deciding whether to reorient ancient Greek to sound like modern English or to try to make a direct word-for-word translation. A direct word-for-word translation may be incredibly difficult to understand for some. Therefore, this leads to different scholars deciding to carefully craft translations based on what they believe they're led to do. This important job requires integrity, honesty, careful study, research, linguistic skill, and anything that aids translation. Thus, this is why many translations exist, such as the KJV, NKJV, NIV, NIRV, NLT, AMP, and so forth.

Again, it is wise to compare translations. Some versions may sound better given preference in writing style and choice of English used while keeping the same meaning as the original text. Others match the original text nearly verbatim besides grammar, spelling, and punctuation.

DIFFERENCES BETWEEN OLD AND NEW

Many have observed that the New Testament shows way more compassion than the Old Testament. A combination of language translation and context from the agreements made between God and the Hebrew people makes the difference, and halves of the Bible are easier to understand. Covenants are agreements made between members, usually with conditions for each side. God promised in the Old Testament that the whole tribe of Israel would be established in the Promised Land (Jerusalem) and be protected against anyone who may oppose them. See Genesis 12:2–3; 17:4–8; Exodus 2:24–25; 3:8. It's important to know via those verses and the surrounding ones that there is a two-way agreement. God demanded that the commandments be followed.

While reading the Old Testament, you realize the Israelites could have been better at keeping their promise. Once you read past 1 and 2 Kings, you find Israel had many more evil rulers than righteous ones. The people sinned more in those days when evil rulers were present. Whenever the Israelites strayed from God, He let suffering occur. He often didn't hold back on His righteous anger either. Israel consistently broke their covenant, but God never canceled it on His side. God is exceptionally patient; the time frame between the exodus and Israel's exile to Babylon extends about twelve hundred years or so. Even so, God never forgot them because He is merciful; they eventually escaped captivity through the prophesied destruction of Babylon.

The laws and standards established in Exodus, Leviticus, Numbers, and Deuteronomy are stringent and specific. I think God demanded such things in the past to show how difficult it was to live by such laws. He ordered a high standard of perfection because God is perfect and holy. Christians often discuss this issue this way when studying: God had a boundary between Him and His people because of sin. The only people who could come close to His presence in the tabernacle by law were priests and leaders like Moses. People often died on the spot if regulations weren't met. The Hebrews were always warned ahead of time; there wasn't any excuse for breaking God's law because they had agreed to terms after leaving Egypt. It was a relatively small price to pay to be free from long persecution in Egypt. It is suspected that they were there for over four hundred years.

The point here is that the Old Testament doesn't quite finish the story on purpose. What about all the unfulfilled prophecies? Not everything foretold was fulfilled before the era of Christ. If we only ever had the Old Testament, we'd all still be subject to the law of Moses. We'd still have to make animal sacrifices, be stoned for offenses, eat a specific diet, and much more. The law leaves more to be desired, needing fulfillment. The Old Testament is a preamble containing impossible standards through human effort pointing to something greater. It also includes excellent wisdom through outstanding accounts, poetry, and proverbs; and it foretells hope.

THE LONG GAME STRATEGY

God certainly planned ahead because I see the following pattern in the Old Testament:

- God makes it impossible for humans to follow the law to completion.
- People who manage to follow it to their best ability through faith ought to be blessed.
- If most people decide to turn away from Him, He appropriately provides consequences.
- He lets a long period pass before making a new promise. He shows by example that what we do will never be enough.
- God establishes a new contract through a perfect sacrifice capable of fulfilling the law through Jesus.

Hebrews 11 in the New Testament talks about many people in the Old Testament who followed God to their best ability because they had faith in Him. Faith was always God's plan from the beginning. First, Adam was given authority over the creatures of the earth. He was also given a helper suitable for him in the form of a woman, made from his flesh. There was no reason to distrust God when He said in Genesis 2:16–17, "But the Lord God warned him, 'You may freely eat the fruit of every tree in the garden. except the tree of the knowledge of good and evil. If you eat of its fruit, you are sure to die.'" Things today would be perfect if they had denied their pleasure, trusted God in what He said (another way to say faith), and informed God of the deceiver. A straightforward test was put before the first people, and they failed miserably because that is human nature.

Later, God showed the Israelites that He could do great things if they only trusted Him. Yes, there were a lot of moments where they turned their backs on Him, but God never wholly forgot them.

2

PROMISES AND
SUFFERING

L et's talk about the complex topic of suffering. Suffering is a big reason people refuse to trust in God. Suffering is the most challenging topic because God allows suffering during our short time on earth, but it isn't for fun and has a purpose. I will also speak about a particular mistake we often make because I make them too. The Bible says that if we claim we don't sin, we are liars (1 John 1:8–10).

I admit that the Old Testament is dark regarding what took place. There is no denying that many deaths, diseases, turmoil, and suffering occurred before Christ. There was certainly a fair share of those in the New Testament, but comparatively speaking, the Old Testament is known for brutality by modern definition. I agree to a point, but there is a reason for everything. Let's address the subject of God's agreement and societal destruction.

THE LORD'S PROMISE: A NEW
HOME AND PROTECTION

There is no way to sugarcoat the fact that Israel nearly obliterated many ancient nations with the direct help of God Almighty. The Bible clearly states that men, women, and children were killed; this is a fact that rubs people the wrong way. Surrounding nations (Hittites, Amorites, Perizzites, Hivites, and Jebusites) and Israelites were disciplined because of their sins. Hebrew armies fought and killed many in battle. In contrast, some Hebrews weren't allowed in the Promised Land (I mention details in this chapter). It makes complete sense to me why people think the carnage from these accounts is abhorrent.

War is always a touchy subject. Certainly, I'm not too fond of the idea myself, but it is a reality I've come to accept through deeper study. Nothing was done randomly and with complete disregard for life. The Bible is very plain and straightforward about how important His people are. Exodus 23:22 says, "But if you are careful to obey Him, following all My instructions, then I will be an enemy to your enemies, and I will oppose those who oppose you." God would stand up for the Hebrew people if they followed His instructions. God always follows through with His promises. The next verses provide even better context for the demand of destruction. Exodus 23:23–24 says, "For my angel will go before you and bring you into the land of the Amorites, Hittites, Perizzites, Canaanites, Hivites, and Jebusites, so you may live there. You must not worship the gods of these nations or serve them in any way or imitate their evil practices. Instead, you must utterly destroy them and smash their sacred pillars." The key point here is that the surrounding nations had already been corrupted to the point that God was incredibly furious with them.

If we look back at Sodom and Gomorrah as an example, Genesis 18:20 says, "So the Lord told Abraham, 'I have heard a great outcry from Sodom and Gomorrah, because their sin is so flagrant.'" Later, we see descriptions of actual sins being committed in Genesis 19:4–9. All the men of Sodom, young and old, demanded to have intercourse with the "men" (angels) Lot had brought into his house. They would have broken the door down and forced themselves on the "men" if not for the power God granted to them.

So why bother with obliteration, right? That seems like literal overkill to many. God set an unwavering example with Egypt. Pharaoh was stubborn and given many chances to let the Hebrews go. God brought plagues, but each time, Pharaoh eventually said no. There were times when he first agreed but went back on his word. The last plague was the most horrifying. Pharaoh's hard heart led to a terrifying result: the firstborn sons would die if no lamb's blood was found on the door thresholds. This activity established a way to cover sins through the law. The law in later books describes that either lambs or goats with no blemishes would be the prime choice for sacrifice. Moses gave a warning each time beforehand, but the foolish king didn't listen. God was already incredibly angry because Pharaoh had demanded that many Hebrew children be killed along with the people being put to even harder, oppressive work. The time for patience was over. Egypt suffered from Pharaoh's ignorance toward God. God declared war on Egypt. Casualties were now inevitable because His justice was against the waste of life of Hebrew children and people. God had had enough of the oppression.

The surrounding clans or nations already knew what had occurred, along with knowing who God was. They already knew they could turn from their evil ways. Numbers 14:13–16 confirms that the surrounding nations already knew the Lord was with Israel for two reasons: the pillar of cloud in the day and the pillar of fire at night. The other reason is that Egypt's plagues were so drastic that they would have been hard not to notice; the news would have been passed around by word of mouth like wildfire.

Not only that, but the same chapter in Numbers is also about internal rebellion. Some of the Hebrews desired to go back to Egypt. The Lord didn't decide to obliterate these people immediately but instead didn't allow them to enter the Promised Land. This means they died out in the wilderness alone—men, women, and children included. God disciplines even His people and doesn't leave anyone out. It was only suitable to exclude those people from the Promised Land if they didn't want to go. Would it be fair if God spared some over others? The other members of surrounding tribes that didn't rebel would see this and say, "Why was this person spared? Weren't they part of a family that decided to go against God?" The same thing applies to the nations around them. What would be fair and proper? God was also letting the people suffer the consequence of not wanting to go to a better place. Israel didn't follow through with complete obliteration anyway. Second Chronicles 8:7–8 says, "There were still some people living in the land who were not Israelites, including the Hittites, Amorites, Perizzites, Hivites, and Jebusites. These were descendants of the nations whom the people of

Israel had not destroyed. So Solomon conscripted them for his labor force, and they serve as forced laborers to this day." They didn't even fulfill what God had demanded.

A common theme in the Old Testament is that God limits His patience and punishes any nation that stands against Him for a long time. God's standards are absolute: evil is evil, and good is good. The wages of sin is always death (Genesis 3:19, 22–23; Romans 6:23). God has no tolerance for sin (Psalm 5:4). Those nations also desired to destroy anybody in the Hebrew group since there were many attacks recorded. God pays back what would have occurred to His people or what did occur. Many women, children, and vulnerable people died from war and hatred from outside nations.

QUESTION 4: WHAT ABOUT THE KILLING OF WOMEN AND CHILDREN? ISN'T THAT EVIL?

We ought to realize that our definitions and standards don't meet God's definitions and standards (Isaiah 55:8–9). The record of death is hard for anyone to swallow. What we think of as innocence is way off from how God defines it. God knows that true innocence means one is capable of having no sin. There can be no sin present in an innocent person. Children are included because everyone is born with sin. Sadly, many children died in those days, even those who probably couldn't understand right and wrong. God is certainly not against punishing people with highly heavy consequences like this. Consider David's example when he slept with Bathsheba and sent her husband to die. God inflicted an illness on one of his youngest, and David mourned and constantly prayed that God would heal him. Tragically, the child died, but the shocking part is seen in 2 Samuel 12:19–21. David did what nobody expected by getting up, cleansing himself, worshipping, and praising God. He then said in verses 22–23, "I fasted and wept while the child was alive, for I said, 'Perhaps the Lord will be gracious to me and let the child live.' But why should I fast when he is dead? Can I bring him back again? I will go to him one day, but he cannot return to me." The targeting of children always seems cruel because we often think of them as innocent.

According to scripture, nobody is innocent because all are capable of sin. However, God does seem to differentiate us from young ones by acknowledging that young children are incapable of knowing they are sinful. Is it correct to send someone to eternal torment if he or she cannot understand why? Here we can find hope that God doesn't pass judgment on those who cannot possibly know they are capable of sinning. Christians like to talk about this as an "age of accountability." I suggest it could be flexible depending on the person too. If the person is born with mental slowness, it may take longer to understand why what he or she does is wrong. There are even cases where a brain may never be capable of recognizing this. God is a fair and perfect Judge, since He is the Judge above all judges. I want to think that the point at which children are accountable is when they are conscious of their actions. I admit that I don't have the mind of God, so I don't fully know the answer. I do trust that God knows best and will do what is right according to His standards.

People also find it unfair that women were also killed under the direction and help of God in the Old Testament. We have to realize all adults are held accountable for their actions. There is no such thing as a truly "innocent" woman or man. Women can make just as many mistakes as men. (I discuss later in chapter 3 that a woman was tempted first.) The death of children is much harder to accept, as I've discussed in the last paragraph. Without proper context and logical thinking, this sounds cruel at face value. I don't want to appear insensitive by outright justifying without providing reasons.

Let's explore a few questions that might aid the thinking process. First, why would God demand this death? Second, what level of corruption did the surrounding nations have? These questions are related because there is precedent. Pharaoh was given several chances during the plagues until God decided to no longer show patience and cast a death sentence on their firstborn. I suggest that if God demanded the destruction of the evil nations, this implies that His patience had also ended for them. God had declared war on the wicked nations for good reasons.

Third, how oppressed were the Hebrew people for God to declare war? There was a history of nations attacking first without provocation. Exodus 17:8 says, "While the people of Israel were still at Rephidim, the warriors of Amalek attacked them." These other people weren't just petty either. They devastated the Hebrew people in Judges 6:3–5. "Whenever the Israelites planted their crops, marauders from Midian, Amalek, and the people of the east would attack Israel, camping in the land and destroying crops as far away as Gaza. They left the Israelites with nothing to eat, taking all the sheep, goats, cattle, and donkeys. These enemy hordes, coming with their livestock and tents, were as thick as locusts; they arrived on droves of camels too numerous to count. And they stayed until the land was stripped bare." Multiple groups banded together numerous times and plundered their belongings. It hardly seems like they would be willing to negotiate anything. Imagine the sheer number of people in these armies! Language such as "thick as locusts" and "camels were like grains of sand on the seashore—too many to count!" is used! (See Judges 7:12.) Gideon, by comparison, had only three hundred men. It wasn't a fair match by any measure.

Fourth, what responsibility did the Hebrew people have? Fifth, who would dare stand against God's demands? For a moment, let's focus on the situation. Some Hebrew families had already been oppressed in some way by these nations. Many were poor and starving. Logically speaking, these families would then be forced to take responsibility for these foreign children. The addition would add an awful lot of burden to an already-overburdened family. How could this be fair for anyone trying to escape oppression and stress? They all wanted to be taken care of in the Promised Land while filled with nourishment and without the fear of looming murder threats by the massive armies. Then look at the patterns in the Old Testament once more when it comes to punishment for disobedience. Israel had a habit of disobeying and paying dearly, even to the point of death (yes, again this included all ages and types of people too). The people in Joshua's time were so loyal that they made an oath to be put to death if they refused to do what was demanded in Joshua 1:18. "Anyone who rebels against your orders and does not obey your words and everything you command will be put to death. So be strong and courageous!" There was a long period where Israel was oppressed by everyone surrounding them, who intended death and destruction. God was always around to stand up for them in their time of need by providing the ultimate judgment.

Here is a final perspective that might help us come to terms with collateral human destruction in the Old Testament. The children who had surpassed the age of understanding right from wrong were influenced by their parents, who refused to turn to God. They were being taught evil and practiced only evil. They would have been told what the Hebrews believed or had it hidden from them because of hatred. The parents were responsible for their children in this case, and those children would have been capable of making moral decisions. They might not have had complete agency because of their brain development, but at this point, they would have ended up like their parents. We know that some people were spared, based on 2 Chronicles, so it is plausible that some were taught the ways of the Hebrew nation. Others died because they were already corrupted with sin and wouldn't yield.

Everyone is subject to death; some die before they can live a full life. The tragic event of young death today isn't comparable in the same way because we don't have the same circumstances. The exodus was a particular point in time in which oppression was rampant. There may be wars where children die today, but this isn't for similar reasons. The passing away of children isn't necessarily a sign of punishment either. There are many cases in which they pass away due to the curse on the earth. Illness can always affect anyone.

QUESTION 5: WHY DOES GOD ALLOW GOOD PEOPLE TO SUFFER?

I cannot deny that there are better followers than I am, and they can live better than I do in my walk with God. One of the most challenging questions is, why does God allow suffering to occur for those who aren't doing anything wrong? There are so many situations that make people bitter so they choose not to believe anymore. I can understand the feeling because I went through many hard times when I wanted to walk away. My situation was certainly not as excruciating as those other people often experience. I don't want to trivialize those situations by any means.

Look at one of the most heartbreaking books of the Bible. Job was a mighty man of God the Bible says was blameless. The devil asked God if he could prove that Job would crack under pressure and curse God if God took everything Job had. God agreed to this proposal, knowing that Job wouldn't curse Him. I have heard many people say this was God making a bet on Job and readily letting this strong man go through awful stuff for fun. If you read the whole book, you will find a different case. God wasn't having a joy ride by playing a game with the devil. God knew who Job was and understood his character perfectly. Job stayed true to everything he believed in and eventually made a mistake near the end of the book by being arrogant.

My point is that God doesn't delight in suffering. Here are verses to back up that claim. Ezekiel 18:23–24 says, "Do you think that I like to see wicked people die? Says the Sovereign Lord. Of course not! I want them to turn from their wicked ways and live. However, if righteous people turn from their righteous behavior and start doing sinful things and act like other sinners, should they be allowed to live? No, of course not! All their righteous acts will be forgotten, and they will die from their sins." Surely if God cares for sinners this much, He cares just as much for those who believe. Later in the New Testament, Jesus discovered that Mary's brother Lazarus was dying. Mary was the woman who had used her hair to wipe perfume on His feet. Jesus couldn't make it quite in time before Lazarus passed away. John 11:33–35 says, "Jesus saw the woman weeping and the other people wailing with her, a deep anger welled up within Him, and he was deeply troubled. 'Where have you put him?' He asked them. They told Him, 'Lord, come and see.' Then Jesus wept." I think some of those emotions are both from people's disbelief and simply feelings from seeing people grieve their beloved one. Christians believe Jesus and God the Father are the same. God can feel the same way if we suffer, for He became human.

I propose there are a lot of reasons for suffering. Isaiah 48:8, 10–11 shows that God may punish those doing something wrong and calls suffering a "refinement process" by giving an "anti-analogy" of sorts to how silver is refined in the fire. I'm not saying this is always the case; God can prevent or let things happen naturally. We still live in a world full of disease, death, chaos, and evil due to the curse He put on the world due to sin. Sometimes bad things happen; it's okay to feel angry at this time. I don't think God wants us to either lose hope or become depressed. It is tough to accept what has happened and turn your perspective around. God never said things would be easy for us. Ecclesiastes 3 describes that there is a time for good and a time for evil. There are different seasons in life. Would we truly have free will if God prevented every possible negative thing? Worse yet, wouldn't that make God a liar by going back on His word? God had to curse the world because Adam and Eve made sinful choices. They could have accepted God's instruction, but they turned and made their own choice based on what felt good to them.

Finally, what if worse things were to happen to those who pass away? There can be far worse things than dying, especially for those who believe. As a simple example, some catastrophic events could have caused them worse pain. Isaiah 57:1–2 says, "Good people pass away; the godly often die before their time. But no one seems to care or wonder why. No one seems to understand that God is protecting them from the evil to come. For those who follow godly paths will rest in peace when they die." We don't have anything to worry about if we follow God.

WE CAN BE WRONG ABOUT HARD TIMES

It can be extremely difficult to know when to sympathize and when to counsel. I think as Christians we tend to try to bring about meaning to things before anything else. We often try to say the right thing with the best intentions, but we aren't doing it at the right time. Maybe some people are comforted by a greater meaning to extremely difficult hardships like losing a loved one to cancer, losing a baby, experiencing heartbreak, going through depression—you name it. However, others may not be built the same way. Some people hear that message and think, *How condescending and uncaring is that!* We ought to ask how people are feeling first and see if they just need someone to be there and grieve with them instead of hearing counsel. Learning to gauge how people might react is a good skill to have.

I advise being in grief before anything else, giving time and space when needed, and then asking them if they'd like to be encouraged by what you think. Never do what many young Christians or hypocrites do by accusing people of sinning when they go through tragedy. We aren't the judge at this moment (Matthew 7:1–2) and have no right to tell others they must be wrong. This instance isn't the time or place for any casting blame. It is always an individual's responsibility to make peace with God and search them are justified. Luke 23:39–43 says, "One of the criminals hanging beside him scoffed, 'So you're the Messiah, are you? Prove it by saving yourself—and us, too, while you're at it!' But the other criminal protested, 'Don't you fear God even when you have been sentenced to die? We deserve to die for our crimes, but this man hasn't done anything wrong.' Then he said, 'Jesus, remember me when you come into your Kingdom.' And Jesus replied, 'I assure you, today you will be with me in paradise.'" Two attitudes are shown in this passage. One is scoffing and goading. That man didn't admit anything; he wasn't humble enough to recognize his sin. The other realized they both deserved to die for their crimes while seeing Jesus as truly innocent because He was God. His heart changed while he was slowly dying. His desperate plea for Jesus to remember him was a cry for forgiveness. Yes, even people who have done wrong for their entire lives can be redeemed near the end if in their hearts they acknowledge how wicked they've been. The gospel is for everyone. It is good news for all who are willing to believe He forgives their sins.

CHARACTER BUILDING, BOLSTERING FAITH

I genuinely think God wants what is best for us, but only He knows what that actually is. If we stray from what He wants, He may give more than a gentle nudge back toward it. After all, do we not learn from our parents through discipline? We might not like it at the moment, but when we are older, we look back and realize we have changed for the better due to discipline. I'm definitely not by any means saying tough love is easy to accept.

On the other hand, it's not always something we do wrong either. Again, hard times occur with no apparent reason to us; that is reality. There are great things that can come out of suffering. Let me illustrate it this way; imagine someone has just lost a loved one due to cancer. He or she is grieving, thinks the world is lost, and doesn't initially have anyone to relate to. God works through people as family members and friends hear of this terrible tragedy. Immediately, this person is showered with all the love he or she could possibly want or need. People start doing things for this person, people offer comfort, people grieve with him or her, and some for any possible wrongdoing on his or her own time (which might not be the case anyway). We also forget scripture in its proper context when being put on the spot. Being a Christian isn't supposed to have a holier-than-thou attitude but rather a guilty-as-charged attitude. A person who is in the right relationship with God will recognize his or her own faults before anything else. We cannot know a person's life by what happens to him or her. God either causes things directly or lets nature take place because the curse of the world is still at hand. We don't know which is the case and cannot possibly know because we don't know God's intricate plan in depth.

QUESTION 6: WHY DOES GOD PUNISH? ISN'T HE ALWAYS LOVING?

Christians think of God as the perfect Father because He has made us, comforts us, leads us, and does everything a good father should to perfection. It's easy to believe or feel that your parents must enjoy punishing you just to exercise power over you. There are, of course, examples of negligent, abusive, and inadequate parents who don't treat their children properly. For the most part, however, parents want the best for their children. If I think about it, I can imagine it is challenging for a parent to impart some form of misery on his or her children. If I was a parent, I wouldn't like my children to be sad, angry, or upset —or ideally to experience anything negative. The reality is, to properly raise children, discipline is required. The Bible backs this up in Deuteronomy 8:5. "Think about it: Just as a parent disciplines a child, the Lord your God disciplines you for your own good." So God certainly disciplines those who disobey His commands. We might not love this discipline when it's happening, but if we grow up in that environment, we realize it is eventually for our own good.

The statement "God is love" is truthful, but many forget that He has more attributes. He is not only love but also true, just, righteous, holy, and so on. Suppose everyone did go to heaven. What about justice against atrocities committed by those who felt they did no wrong? How fair would it be to allow serial killers with no remorse into a perfect world simply because they are human? The New Testament states that people whose hearts acknowledge their evil for what it is and believe Jesus can forgive may even contribute great gifts. I could go on and on about how much love can be poured into this. To my memory, Randy Alcorn, one of my favorite writers, says this: "The statement God is love in the Bible is more significant than we know. Logically speaking, this means that any form of legitimate love is coming directly from God. Whether it is love from your friends, husband or wife, strangers, you name it. Love is from God. God is the very essence of love." I sincerely recommend reading *If God Is Good* by Randy Alcorn because I believe this concept is described in that book. The book definitely helped me see a different perspective on suffering. Romans 8:28 pretty much sums up this chapter: "And we know that God causes everything to work together for the good of those who love God and are called according to his purpose for them."

3

OPPRESSION OR PROTECTION?

God's law is often described as oppressive, restrictive, unfair, and unjust. It is incredibly touchy when it comes to three topics in the Bible. The first is the view that the Bible restricts women far more than it does men. The second is the issue of slavery, which has been abolished in the modern day but existed in biblical times. The third is restrictions on sexual relations.

Yes, there were different regulations for men and women. This doesn't mean things were unfair or oppressive from God's perspective. It can be easy to feel like this if you keep certain verses in your head and don't consider others. The Bible is a very long book. It is challenging to remember what was said. People also conflate or mix cultural practices recorded in history with scripture. Historical context matters, however; there is an argument to be made that it wasn't meant to be so oppressive. Unfortunately, that is how ancient society often behaved. People distorted God's law, and their practices flew in the face of what He demanded. If you read the Old Testament, you will find that a lot of what ancient Israel did wasn't pleasing to God; nor did it always follow His law.

TERMS OF THE CURSE

There were specific consequences for Adam and Eve along with their descendants. The Bible records that Eve was the first to be convinced by the devil, who appeared in the form of a serpent. Adam followed by accepting the fruit from Eve that came from the Tree of Knowledge of Good and Evil. God knows this happened, addressed both of them with exact details of how the world was cursed, and explained their respective consequences. Genesis 3:16 says, "Then he said to the woman, 'I will sharpen the pain of your pregnancy, and in pain you will give birth. And you will desire to control your husband, but he will rule over you.'" The declaration is precise, and we see the effects throughout the ages. Curses are things not originally meant to be; God wanted them to make the right decision, but of course, they didn't. This suggests that consequences wouldn't have been that way if they hadn't made choices as they did. Women would have either no pain or very little at birth and would be in perfect harmony with their husbands. The man wasn't left out either. Genesis 3:17–19 says, "And to the man he said, 'Since you listened to your wife and ate from the tree whose fruit I commanded you not to eat, the ground is cursed because of you. All your life you will struggle to scratch a living from it. It will grow thorns and thistles for you, though you will eat of its grains. By the sweat of our brow will you have food to eat until you return to the ground from which you were made. For you were made from dust, and to dust you will return.'"

God goes by the order in which things were committed. I don't think this method is by accident. Eve acted first, so God punished her before Adam. Are the punishments really unequal? They sound equally bad to me, considering that life for them wasn't supposed to be that way before sin. Men work with intense labor, the ground grows thorns and thistles, and of course eventually dying sounds just as bad for the man as for the woman. Also, relational problems now exist through the woman's consequences (something that applies to both parties in actuality). The man suffers equally in the sense that there is dissidence between the two. Even if you disagree, I could easily make the case that Eve enticed her husband and committed sin first. Who are we to say that God has to punish equally? After all, we currently have different levels of crime with varying levels of consequences.

QUESTION 7: WHY DOES GOD CURSE
HUMANITY OVER JUST EATING FRUIT?

There is a related argument to the issue of Adam and Eve eating from the tree that I should mention: "Why would God curse the entirety of humankind over eating fruit? Surely I wouldn't have made that mistake." There are two counterarguments I make against this. One, God explicitly instructed both of them not to eat from this tree. God doesn't lie, and what He demands is final. The one who made us ought to have the last say, after all. The task wasn't particularly complex either.

However, I don't think some realize the depth of what happened. My second point is that there is a reason Eve was convinced to eat the fruit. The serpent, Satan, first used a gaslighting method of argument in Genesis 3:1 by saying, "Did God really say you must not eat the fruit from any of the trees in the garden?" Eve corrected the serpent by giving an accurate statement and saying only one specific tree was off limits. However, the devil came back in Genesis 3:4–5 with, "'You won't die' The serpent replied to the woman. 'God knows that your eyes will be opened as soon as you eat it, and you will be like God, knowing both good and evil.'" The sixth verse says the woman was convinced by this, saw how beautiful the tree was, and ate the fruit. The heart of the matter is this: how tempting would it be to possibly have the ability to know what God knows or be just like God? The issue was pride in the heart, along with not depending on God alone. This is the true source of all sin: doing things without God and disregarding what He desires. Try to put yourselves in that situation and deeply think about the enticement of knowledge and becoming like God. If that had been anyone else, Satan would have used either similar language or language that enticed him or her in the same way.

QUESTION 8: WHY DOES GOD TREAT
WOMEN OPPRESSIVELY?

One verse people argue about is Colossians 3:18. "Wives, submit to your husbands, as is fitting for those who belong to the Lord." Many men and women find the verse offensive because it comes off as demeaning to women. I think this verse is often misconstrued. There are a lot of denominations (or types) of Christianity, and not all of them agree with each other. Some take that instruction super literally and demand that women are subservient to men, but I don't think that is what the verse is getting at. The word *submission* can mean something deeper and more loving. My upbringing views it as an act of respect to the man of the household. There is more to the instruction anyway, which seems to be ignored in this context. Colossians 3:19 says, "Husbands, love your wives and never treat them harshly." Marriage is also supposed to be a reflection of the relationship between Jesus and His church. Jesus sacrificed everything for His bride.

Respect is a two-way street. You can't just demand it from one side. I don't think it's right to treat anyone less than human. Men shouldn't treat women as if they weren't human. That isn't loving and is especially abusive. Being submissive isn't the same thing as being completely subservient. In ancient times, it was culturally acceptable to be a little more strict about this. Women had a lesser role than men, but from what I've read in the Bible, they weren't treated as less than human by any standard. Let me provide a few examples of strong, faithful women in the Old Testament, whom their fellow men respected.

INTEGRAL WOMEN IN THE OLD TESTAMENT

There are many examples of women in the Bible who held important roles, even in the Old Testament. In the book of Joshua, a woman named Rahab directly helped some spies sent into Jericho. Here is something surprising; despite the laws established through God's teaching, which clearly states adultery isn't allowed, the Bible states that she was a prostitute. Rahab helped the men by hiding them from officials who were looking for them. Rahab admitted that she had heard of the Lord's power through the splitting of the Red Sea. She called the Lord "the supreme God of the heavens above and the earth below." Rahab requested that the men be kind to her and her family since she had saved them. They in turn offered their lives to guarantee her safety. This story comes from Joshua 2:1–14. Normally, it was required to stone people guilty of prostitution, but the Lord was merciful to those who turned from their sinful ways. The Israelites adopted her and her family into their society. Joshua 6:25 says, "So Joshua spared Rahab the prostitute and her relatives who were with her in the house because she had hidden the spies Joshua sent to Jericho. And she lives among the Israelites to this day." This news flies in the face of the idea that women are treated poorly in the Bible. The men respected this woman and followed through with their promise. Not only that, but Rahab is mentioned in the lineage of Jesus! Matthew 1:5 says, "Salmon was the father of Boaz (whose mother is Rahab). Boaz was the father of Obed (whose mother is Ruth). Obed was the father of Jesse." Jesse is David's father, and his lineage led to Jesus.

Not too long after Rahab is mentioned, a woman named Deborah is given a vital role in the book of Judges. Before the nation of Israel had any kings, they depended on judges who stood as arbiters for the Lord. The book of Judges explains that Israel went back and forth, doing evil before the Lord. The Lord turned them over to their enemies, the people begged for the Lord's help, and then the Lord provided someone to serve as a rescuer. Deborah was fourth in line to serve as a judge for the Lord. The Bible even says she was a prophet. Judges 4:4 says, "Deborah, the wife of Lappidoth, was a prophet who was judging Israel at that time." Deborah prophesied that the Israelites would have victory over the Canaanites, who had oppressed them for twenty years. Judges 4:1–3 says, "After Ehud's death, the Israelites again did evil in the Lord's sight. So the Lord turned them over to King Jabin of Hazor, a Canaanite king. The commander of his army was Sisera, who lived in Harosheth-haggoyim. Sisera, who had 900 iron chariots, ruthlessly oppressed the Israelites for twenty years. Then the people of Israel cried out to the Lord for help." Not only did Deborah predict victory, but she provided peace in the land for forty years. See Judges 5:31: "'Lord, may all your enemies die like Sisera! But may those who love you rise like the sun in all its power!' Then there was peace in the land for forty years." A role of significant authority and responsibility was given to a woman. That doesn't seem to me like they had no rights.

I highly encourage you to read the book of Ruth in its entirety. The story is extremely touching and significant to the genealogy of Jesus. In summary, a woman named Naomi lost her husband and her two sons, and she had nobody left. One of her daughters-in-law, Ruth, decided to stick with Naomi regardless of what happened because Ruth loved and cared for her mother-in-law. Ruth 1:16–17 says, "But Ruth replied, 'Don't ask me to leave you and turn back. Wherever you go, I will go; wherever you live, I will live. Your people will be my people, and your God will be my God. Wherever you die, I will die, and there I will be buried. May the Lord punish me severely if I allow anything but death to separate us!'" Ruth was loyal until death. She was blessed because of this decision, ended up marrying Boaz, and had a child named Obed. Naomi cared for this child as her own. Obed was the father of Jesse, the father of David. Again, David's lineage goes all the way forward to Jesus. Gracious women started a long process that would lead to the birth of our Savior. It was essential to the utmost degree that this path took place.

One of my favorite books has ten chapters about a Hebrew queen named Esther, who married the great king Xerxes. This book can also provide a great example of what submission and love look like from both sides. The king's wicked official, Haman, convinced the king to plot the downfall of the Jewish people in the area. Haman wasn't aware that a Jew named Mordecai had earlier warned Xerxes about a plot against the king. The king confirmed the details of Mordecai's report and held a feast where Haman thought he would be honored, but Mordecai was honored instead. By the end of the book, Haman was executed along with his sons.

It was custom at this time to have people killed who didn't formally request an audience with the king unless he held forward his scepter. Esther never rushed into the courtroom, demanding things with force. She always came in with grace and said, "If it pleases the King" (Esther 5:4; 7:3; 8:5; 9:13). Esther respected her husband by politely requesting things. Xerxes, on the other hand, passionately loved Esther and deeply respected her. He didn't force his way. Rather, the king always provided and made remarks such as this in Esther 5:3. "Then the king asked her, 'What do you want, Queen Esther? What is your request? I will give it to you, even if it is half the kingdom!'" I think the situation would have gone a lot differently if Esther had come in, demanding things right and left by yelling things. I find this book to be a great example of what a relationship should look like between husband and wife. There is mutual respect and love. I'm definitely not saying the man needs to be some king-like person either.

QUESTION 9: DOESN'T THE BIBLE CONDONE
RAPE IN THE OLD TESTAMENT?

Rape is a severe crime and always has been. It sounds like an obvious statement, but there are arguments some make about the Old Testament. A few verses might sound incriminating without the reader knowing the proper context. A lot of angry comments are made about Deuteronomy 22:28–29: "Suppose a man has intercourse with a young woman who is a virgin but is not engaged to be married. If they are discovered, he must pay her father fifty pieces of silver. Then he must marry the young woman because he violated her, and may never divorce her as long as he lives." The argument is that the verses give a pass for raping women and forcing them to marry.

Let's review a historical practice before referring to a law that clarifies this conundrum. It was highly taboo for Hebrews to have relations with anyone who had lost his or her virginity before marriage. After all, this is part of the law. In this matter, of course, it is a different situation. Even though the woman wouldn't be condemned for such circumstances since she didn't sin, the social stigma would have existed. She may have been mistreated because people are imperfect and judgmental. If you don't consider an older law in Exodus, it could have been reasonable to force a commitment from the man in this case (if the man wasn't stoned or killed for his offense anyway) to preserve the dignity of the woman. This marriage would have lasted for the rest of their lives; according to this law, no divorce was allowed. Try to think of it this way: in one sense, it is a strict punishment for the man while trying to maintain respect for the poor woman. The relationship between the two would have been incredibly distant. The marriage would have been a constant reminder that the man had dishonored the woman, and it would have brought great shame to his name. The community would have looked at the relationship in a new light and pitied the woman who went through torment. The woman benefited, while the man didn't by having a resentful wife and being known as someone who had disgraced a community friend.

However, that is only one perspective, of course. Here is an older law from Exodus 22:16–17 that matters for something like this. "If a man seduces a virgin who is not engaged to anyone and has sex with her, he must pay the customary bride price and marry her. But if her father refuses to let him marry her, the man must still pay him an amount equal to the bride price of a virgin." The law applied to cases of consensual and possibly nonconsensual relations. It also showed that it was customary for the father to be the final decision-maker when someone desired to marry a daughter. The father had the right to refuse the marriage and make the man pay the same price regardless, along with no official marriage taking place. The behavior may also have counted as adultery from the man, and he could have been subject to stoning.

I suspect that death as a consequence was far more common in situations that involved this atrocious act. Here are solid examples of this taking place in the Old Testament:

1. See Genesis 34:5, 7, 25–27, 31. The whole chapter is one of the great examples of what people thought of rape in the past. These particular verses describe a man defiling their sister; they killed every man because of this act and angrily replied to Jacob that the man had treated their sister like a prostitute. They weren't saying their sister was a prostitute in the end either. They said that men were treating her like one.

2. See Judges 20:4–6, 12–13, 35. A small civil war started between Israel and the tribe of Benjamin because a group of evil men from that tribe had decided to rape a woman until dawn. The woman ended up dying from this abuse. The Israelites heard about the atrocity because the husband was so distraught after her death that he sent pieces of her body to all the tribes (yes, the story gets that dark). The Israelites decided to go to war over this crime, and many died. The tribe of Benjamin was nearly destroyed. After this, Israel felt terrible in chapter 21 because of the near obliteration and went against God's curse by telling the tribe to steal women during an annual festival for wives. The chapter concludes that this wasn't what God wanted because Judges 21:25 clearly states, "In those days Israel had no king; all the people did whatever seemed right in their own eyes." This means God could have allowed a tribe to fizzle out of existence because He had allowed them to be defeated in such a way in the war in chapter 20. The Bible makes the

distinction between doing "what is right in the Lord's eyes" and "what is right in their own eyes" in the Old Testament.

3. See 2 Samuel 13:14, 16, 19–22, 28–29. David's son Absalom had an extraordinary sister Tamar. Her half-brother Amnon tricked her by pretending to be sick, then forced himself on her and raped her. Tamar was emotionally scarred from this experience and knew some people would find out and treat her poorly. She begged Amnon not to send her away. Tamar was in terrible grief. Absalom found out and was furious with Amnon. He kept quiet about the rape for two years and waited for an opportune moment; he ended up killing Amnon in revenge.

If the guilty weren't killed first, the laws could be enacted as mentioned. The father could agree or disagree with marriage. Also, Deuteronomy 22:25–26 clearly states, "But if the man meets the engaged woman out in the country, and he rapes her, then only the man must die. Do nothing to the young woman; she has committed no crime worthy of death. She is as innocent as a murder victim."

Some read the verses in Deuteronomy and find that they clash with the law stated in Exodus. The wording may seem contradictory since nothing about the old law in Exodus is mentioned. It's important to remember that these laws were written for the historical people of Israel, not us. The people would have known (or ought to have known) the law because it was the job of the leaders and priests to practice and teach. In modern court, laws written a long time ago still apply and are often used in court as counterarguments. The same thing happened in ancient times, according to Deuteronomy 17:8–9. "'Suppose a case arises in a local court that is too hard for you to decide—for instance, whether someone is guilty of murder or only of manslaughter, or a difficult lawsuit, or a case involving different kinds of assault. Take such legal cases to the place the Lord your God will choose, And present them to the Levitical priests or the judge on duty at that time. They will hear the case and declare the verdict.'" The passage implies that the ancient law is under the judge's discretion and open to interpretation, just as modern law is. In other words, some law isn't exhaustive but substantive.

Hypothetically speaking, I can imagine a situation like this: Suppose a woman who wasn't engaged reported that a particular man had raped her. In the time of Deuteronomy, the priest may have initially declared that the man had to marry her. She protested this, and so did her father. They said, "Do you remember the old law after our exodus from Egypt? It says that the father has the right to deny marriage and demand payment from the wicked man!" The priest looked in the law, found what was recorded, and agreed with it. It was also the priest's duty to ask God to verify claims because people could lie. Once God affirmed this, the priest probably declared that the old law took precedence. There might also have been a case made against the man, in which the father accused him of adultery. I can imagine that might also have been agreed with, and the man was subject to death by stoning. Laws were nuanced and required arbitration, just like today. Laws were subject to interpretation, and indeed the priests would have gone to God for help.

QUESTION 10: THE BIBLE ALSO CONDONES SLAVERY. ISN'T SLAVERY EVIL?

If what I'm writing isn't clear, I am showing that it isn't fair to judge an ancient society in terms of modern society. Ancient times often don't compare to what we experience now. Christians often get treated as if we still believe all the old practices should be in place, but that is definitely not true. What Christians should understand is that some things do change, and some things stay constant. The base Ten Commandments are among some of the things that are universally true in God's eyes. Jesus stated this in the New Testament. Matthew 5:17–19 says, "Don't misunderstand why I have come. I did not come to abolish the law of Moses or the writings of the prophets. No, I came to accomplish their purpose. I tell you the truth, until heaven and earth disappear, not even the smallest detail of God's law will disappear until its purpose is achieved. So if you ignore the least commandment and teach others to do the same, you will be called the least in the Kingdom of Heaven. But anyone who obeys God's laws and teaches them will be called great in the Kingdom of Heaven." Jesus meant that His death would be able to fulfill all the law demanded of people and that it didn't just disappear. God's people ought to teach and practice the law. I acknowledge old laws and find their purpose. At the same time, I'm not convicted by some of the obscure ones, like eating a particular food or not cutting hair. They don't cause me to hate people or God. We can't completely follow the law without Him anyway.

Slavery is one example of a practice that is no longer permitted because it goes against the idea of loving people. Matthew 18:18 says, "I tell you the truth, whatever you forbid on earth will be forbidden in heaven, and whatever you permit on earth will be permitted in heaven." Christians fought to end slavery in the abolition days because it simply didn't fit what was right. This is an excellent example of fulfilling the law to its ultimate purpose.

The harsh reality is that slavery existed in the ancient world and was widely accepted. However, I can point out that it wasn't always the same as what we think of now. From reading throughout the Old Testament, we see that slaves were treated almost like family members because they were required to follow the law like anyone else. Egypt didn't treat the Hebrews remotely as well as the law demanded. This treatment would probably be more comparable to what we think of slavery today. God demanded that Hebrew "owned" slaves were to be treated fairly. The entire chapter of Exodus 21 describes some of the requirements the Hebrew people had to follow for enslaved people. Look at Exodus 21:4–6. "If his master gave him a wife while he was a slave and they had sons or daughters, then only the man will be free in the seventh year, but his wife and children will still belong to his master. But the slave may declare, 'I love my master, my wife, and my children. I don't want to go free.' If he does this, his master must present him before God. Then his master must take him to the door or doorpost and publicly pierce his ear with an awl. After that the slave will serve his master for life." This hints that the Hebrews ought to have treated their slaves with respect and dignity because they were still people, not simply objects or property. Verse 4 might sound weird, but what man doesn't love his wife and children? Wouldn't it have been wicked for that man to leave his wife and children to be alone with someone else? Besides, if the master treated them in a wicked manner, they'd go free too. Exodus 21:26–27 backs this up. "If a man hits his male or female slave in the eye and the eye is blinded, he must let the slave go free to compensate for the eye. And if a man knocks out the tooth of his male or female slave, he must let the slave go free to compensate for the tooth." This is a pretty straightforward verse; slaves were to be treated as people and even set free if injured severely. Brutality wasn't allowed, even for enslaved people. See Deuteronomy 23:15–16. "If slaves should escape from their masters and take refuge with you, you must not hand them over to their masters. Let them live among you in any town they choose, and do not oppress them." God doesn't tolerate wickedness against anyone. Period.

One verse that may be taken poorly is Leviticus 19:20. "If a man has sex with a slave girl whose freedom has never been purchased but who is committed to become another man's wife, he must pay full compensation to her master. But since she is not a free woman, neither the man nor the woman will be put to death." It is important to know that the man still had to compensate regardless of the person's status. It is also important that the word *rape* isn't used here, so this implies a consensual relationship. There was no free rein on women, even enslaved ones, then. There were still consequences.

As already stated, slavery was a cultural practice that was accepted at the time. If we had lived during that time, we wouldn't have batted an eye because we would have grown accustomed to all these regulations. We would have been cast out of society, killed, or denounced if we had gone against anything demanded by the law. It is also possible that the law would have been ignored based on Israel's troubling cycle of disobedience too. Ignoring God's law isn't the lawmaker's fault but the fault of imperfect people doing evil. History is filled with inconvenient truths and practices we see as reprehensible now. We ought to focus on what is taking place now. If we look at the Sermon on the Mount in Matthew, we will see that abolishing slavery is taking the law to its ultimate purpose. This shows love to people in the form of no longer being able to own a person. Let them be free from any obligation they didn't agree to.

QUESTION 11: WHY IS THE BIBLE
SEXUALLY OPPRESSIVE?

The Bible clearly states that sex is designated only for a married man and woman. God designed us to procreate since He commanded to be fruitful and multiply. It is correct that polygamy was permissible in Old Testament times, but this doesn't mean God approved of it. People couldn't just do whatever they wanted outside of the marriage relationship. Genesis 2:23–25 says, "'At last!' the man exclaimed. 'This one is bone from my bone, and flesh from my flesh! She will be called "woman," because she was taken from "man."' This explains why a man leaves his father and mother and is joined to his wife, and the two are united into one. Now the man and his wife were both naked, but they felt no shame." Then in Leviticus 18:22, we see, "Do not practice homosexuality, having sex with another man as with a woman. It is a detestable sin." Even in the New Testament, it is mentioned again because there is still significance to sexual immorality. Our bodies are meant to be temples for the Holy Spirit; we shouldn't defile them with these acts. See Romans 1:26–27; 1 Corinthians 6:9; and 1 Timothy 1:10–11 for New Testament examples. The Bible also shows a distinction between a man and a woman in Genesis.

The vast problem many Christians fail to recognize is that we have no right to judge people unfairly, and we should be ashamed if we hate anyone who does something against what we believe. We are guilty of sin by hating anyone. We aren't supposed to condemn people. We can hate what is done in action, but we must show compassion, kindness, mercy, and love to those doing it. It isn't our responsibility or right to decide for others. The change must be made internally for each unique individual. The tricky part for most zealous followers is separating people from actions. God loves the person, not the sin living in us.

On the other hand, compassion and mercy don't always mean being nice. We come back to the concept of tough love. Through God's help, we can be wholly compassionate and merciful while providing counterarguments. There are also a time and place for everything. Public ridicule serves only to embarrass the other party. We should be sincere in talking to people one-on-one while acting as Christ did. We should listen to people and try to see their perspectives before doing anything. We need to note why they think the way they do. I am guilty of jumping to criticism instead of hearing someone out, and I deeply regret things I've said in anger. Is there love when we disregard a person entirely? Is there compassion when showering someone with criticism? We cannot be belligerent. Belligerence isn't loving. We can say, "This is wrong because

God says it isn't right." We should never say, "You are wrong for doing this." There is a significant difference between these phrases: pointing out an action as wrong versus indictment and judgment on an individual who is just like us. We have to be very clear that we are only stating what the Word says and tread carefully to avoid forms of language that make us seem disdainful of people.

QUESTION 12: WHY DOES THE BIBLE HAVE SO MANY INSIGNIFICANT, NITPICKY RULES?

Many laws seem like little details that are nitpicks in the modern view. Why restrict what can be eaten? Why restrict what should be cleaned and what is considered unclean? Why does it matter when sexual intercourse occurs? I have a few perspectives on this issue. First, God demands purity in His presence. Second, health standards were nearly nonexistent. Environmental conditions then were much worse than in our modern day. There were no hospitals, no modern medicine, and there were little to no sterilization processes. When I read the restrictions on what should and shouldn't be eaten, why having sex during a woman's period isn't allowed, and when you should clean your house or consider it condemned, I don't see restrictions for oppression. I see God's concern for ancient Israel's health. God also doesn't hate the animals He created (He made them, after all). However, He knows the potential diseases they may carry. The third reason is that God can restrict whatever He likes. God isn't saying that being "ceremonially unclean" is a sin, but not preparing yourself with proper self-care before going into God's presence is. Lastly, the New Testament says this in Mark 10:5: "But Jesus responded, 'He wrote this commandment only as a concession to your hard hearts.'" He was specifically talking about divorce, but possibly many other rules fell under this category, too. God may have decided to regulate based on what was on the Israelites' hearts.

PROTECTING THE SOUL AT ALL COSTS

God restricts anything that isn't for our ultimate good. He is the only one who knows what is best for us. There are serious consequences, both physical and spiritual, for these sins. There is a natural consequence for eating something that can make you sick without proper preparation. There are natural consequences such as STDs, mental exasperation, depression, anxiety, and other things that happen when you don't have relations in the way God designed. There were serious health concerns for many things restricted in the Old Testament. God knows everything.

God is also the perfect Judge, as I've said before. He is the only one who knows the law's true extent, and it is only right that the punishment fits the crime. Whether we think it is fair, we cannot be the judge because we don't know what is truly fair and just. Who are we to say it isn't right to have different punishments? Do we not have similar standards with laws we establish? It doesn't matter if a man or woman commits a crime. They ought to receive the appropriate punishment that fits the crime. Even if the sin of Adam and Eve is equivalent in God's eyes, who has the final say on the sentence? Do we get to decide our punishment, or does the judge? Only God determines what ought to be. God also has the absolute right to go against "normal" societal views. You can see this in the "Integral Role of Women" section. The same sentiment is also reflected in the New Testament, where Jesus completely obliterates expectations by saying the law boils down to loving God and people. We should turn the other cheek, not be angry, and pray for our enemies. God had underlying purposes in ancient law not revealed until his Son came. First Corinthians 6:19–20 states that our bodies are temples for the Holy Spirit. He gave us our bodies; we don't belong to ourselves, and He bought us at an immeasurably high price. This chapter has excellent insight into our bodies being set apart for God.

4

RATIONAL AND HISTORICAL

When I read the Bible, I don't see a bunch of lies whipped up by some third party who wants control. There is a belief in a conspiracy theory that some groups came up with all the words found in scripture to control what people do. It is an accurate record of Hebrew and Christian history—truthful in content, full of wisdom, and incredibly thorough. Why do all other sources of historical information have the ability to affirm their knowledge but the Bible can't? I want to show that accuracy was maintained along with being rational.

QUESTION 13: HOW CAN WE TRUST THE BIBLE IF IT CONTAINS "FAIRY TALES"? IT ISN'T HISTORICAL OR RATIONAL.

Historical content must be logical, factual, consistent, and consistent with recorded events. Let's look at evidence that lines up with what the Bible describes. First, most Jews agree that the Old Testament has significance. Many don't believe Jesus is the Messiah. Yet they agree everything Jesus said when quoting the Old Testament was accurate, and everything recorded in the Old Testament is accurate enough to stand up to scrutiny. If an entire group of people finds a significant portion of the Bible valid, how can we say they are simply delusional? However, one can always say there were lies made up. How can it be a bunch of lies if many Muslims agree that Abraham, Isaac, and Jacob existed along with other ancient Hebrews? This may be word of mouth, of course, but the Hebrew and Aramaic languages exist too. Thousands of ancient texts were written on papyrus, tablets, and other mediums in these languages. They, along with records of the words written in the Bible, confirm the existence of the Hebrew people.

The Red Sea was searched, and something astonishing was found: Egyptian chariots from the time of Moses. Roman census documents prove Jesus existed. The fact that physical scripture manuscripts exist is astonishing. Thousands of manuscripts have been verified to be written within a short period of the suspected origin date. The time in which records appear is a very important concept for historicity. Nearly every piece of scriptural writing was written fewer than one hundred years before the expected origin date. By comparison, these documents are "younger" than Homer's *Odyssey*. The manuscripts go as far back as Israel's exodus in 1446 BC. Yes, the world is older according to the Christian timeline. However, this doesn't mean the manuscripts are unreliable since they don't go back to the beginning. How do we know there aren't manuscripts we haven't found or have been destroyed due to the effects of time? Why is the passing down of information by word of mouth not valid? I agree that that form of recordkeeping isn't nearly as verifiable as written records, but what matters is how this is done. The ancient Hebrew people were extremely careful and meticulous in preserving and copying scripture to the point of starting over if a simple word or character wasn't preserved.

LINEAGE DETAIL

Let's look at a few examples of the Old Testament's thoroughness. For brevity's sake, I will refer to verses that contain lineage but won't include them in the verse appendix. These tend to be very long sections that list name after name and list a bunch of intricate details, along with measurements. I advise you to download a free Bible application or purchase a Bible if you don't already have one. I am not trying to hide anything; I want the appendix to be short enough to be a quick reference.

Exodus 6:14–25 covers several generations of ancestors of Aaron and Moses. Many chapters and books cover lineage after lineage and give a detailed record of how many people were in each tribe. The first twelve chapters of Numbers detail how many people were in each tribe of Israel. It also describes what each tribe was supposed to do according to the law. Genealogy isn't just mentioned once either. The first eight chapters of Chronicles also establish many names and numbers. It shows that records were kept and maintained between generations. Many scholars also find that it is credible that these people existed because of the existence of manuscripts.

TABERNACLE ITEMS AND CUSTOMS

Besides the lists of names, there are also specific details of things made for God and details on customs God required. In Exodus, we find many examples of how particular the design of the ark of the covenant was. Exodus 25 talks about details of the tables and lampstands, the creation of the ark, the traditions and customs required within the tabernacle, and the very design of the tabernacle. Chapter 38 contains even more details down to the dimensions and materials used. How could someone have possibly made up the numbers recorded in these books? It is challenging to claim that someone lied about things measured, weighed, and designed if found artifacts share the same characteristics.

TRACES OF CHRIST IN THE OLD TESTAMENT

One of the most convincing lines of evidence is the imagery described in books written long before the time of Christ that share shocking similarities, if not exact details, in the New Testament. I will provide some prophecies described in the books of the prophets after this section. Some details appeared before these books that I argue can't be written off as coincidences.

Let's look at the connection between the exodus of the Hebrew people and Christ. The Hebrew people were enslaved in Egypt for a very long time and were treated with malice and extreme prejudice. Moses was born in Egypt and narrowly escaped death as an infant; the Egyptian ruler demanded that Hebrew babies be thrown in the Nile to the crocodiles. God had enough of the oppression and wanted to deliver His people from Egypt. God instructed Moses to warn Pharaoh that there would be many plagues if "His people would not be let go." Pharaoh was a very hard-hearted, stubborn man who let Egypt suffer terrible plagues such as locusts, boils, blood in the rivers, frog invasions, fire and brimstone from the heavens, famine, and more. Each time, the mighty ruler said he wouldn't let the Hebrews go. The last plague was the worst to come: the angel of death would kill each firstborn son if there was no lamb's blood spread across the door thresholds (a young male goat sufficed if they didn't have one).

I retell the story mentioned in chapter 2 to provide context for the last plague. I don't think it's a coincidence that the Hebrew people had to use a young male lamb or goat. Observe where the blood was to be spread: on the tops and sides of the doors' thresholds. If you were to draw rectangles from left to right and top to bottom from the center of the frames, you would form cross shapes. My father pointed out this powerful mental illustration a while ago. The blood from Jesus's hands and head would have been in the same spot. Jesus is also described as "The Lamb Who Was Slain."

Look at some of the practices described for Israelites during Passover in Exodus 12:46. "Each Passover lamb must be eaten in one house. Do not carry any of its meat outside, and do not break any of its bones." Jesus gave His disciples a commandment in Mark 14:22. "As they were eating, Jesus took some bread and blessed it. Then he broke it in pieces and gave it to the disciples saying, 'Take it, for this is my body.'" Jesus also had no bones broken during His crucifixion. Later in Leviticus 1:9–10, there is another connection: "But the internal organs and the legs must first be washed with water. Then the priest will burn the entire sacrifice on the altar as a burnt offering. It is a special gift, a pleasing aroma to the Lord. 'If the animal you present as a burnt offering is from a flock, it may be either a sheep or a goat, but it must be a male with no defects.'" Jesus had no sin (defects). Water and blood poured out when the soldiers thrust a spear into His side to check if He was dead. Jesus also died on Passover. King David wrote this in Psalm 22:16–18: "My enemies surrounded me like a pack of dogs; an evil gang closes in on me. They have pierced my hands and feet.

I can count all my bones. My enemies stare at me and gloat. They divide my garments among themselves and throw dice for my clothing." God had inspired David to use the exact words that would describe events far in the future about Jesus's death. Psalm 69:21 says, "But instead, they give me poison for food; they offer me sour wine for my thirst." Sour wine was offered to Jesus right before He commended His spirit.

SIGNIFICANT PROPHECIES

You could write a whole book, if not several books, on the amount of prophecy provided in the Bible's prophetic books. These books range from Isaiah to Malachi, seventeen in total. A brief overview of the types of prophecy includes Israel's destruction (temple included), Israel's exile to Babylon, promises of suffering, promises of freedom, the premonition of a Messiah, details of Jesus's message and testament, and more. Even David saw visions from God recorded in some psalms.

For now, I will cover five examples of prophecy (there are hundreds) to keep this book relatively short. Daniel 7 and 8 talk about visions of the end-times in Revelation that leave Daniel terrified and confused. I found it fascinating that Daniel was shown something John, a modern disciple, was shown visions of. It is a brief example but still a strong case that God remains consistent. He showed a final revelation to two men of very different ages.

Jesus's disciples often referred to the Old Testament when they recognized an event in the Gospels of Matthew, Mark, Luke, and John. They always used phrases like "This was in order to fulfill prophecy" and then provide verses from the Old Testament. First, Matthew lists the lineage of Jesus back to Abraham. David must be listed in that lineage because of 2 Samuel 7:12–13. "For when you die and are buried with your ancestors, I will raise up one of your descendants, your own offspring, and I will make his kingdom strong. He is the one who will build a house—a temple—for my name. And I will secure his royal throne forever." See Isaiah 9:7 as well: "His government and its peace will never end. He will rule with fairness and justice from the throne of his ancestor David for all eternity. The passionate commitment of the Lord of Heaven's Armies will make this happen!" Although many Jews disregard these because Jesus never established a physical kingdom, they don't realize that domains don't necessarily have to be set in this world. There is an unseen kingdom that lasts forever. Eventually, in Revelation, John was given visions that the current heaven and earth would pass away. In the true sense, a permanent kingdom will be established in the new heaven and earth. Prophecy often applies to current events and things that haven't happened yet.

Jesus's resurrection is mentioned a few times in the Old Testament. Psalm 2:7–8 says, "The king proclaims the Lord's decree: 'The Lord said to me, "You are my son. Today I have become your Father. Only ask, and I will give you the nations as your inheritance, the whole earth as your possession."'" The New Testament says in Acts 13:29–33, "When they had done all the prophecies said about Him, they took Him down from the cross and placed Him in a tomb. But God raised Him from the dead! And over a period of many days He appeared to those who had gone with Him from Galilee to Jerusalem. They are now his witnesses to the people of Israel. And now we are here to bring you this Good News. The promise was made to our ancestors, And God has now fulfilled it for us, their descendants, by raising Jesus. This is what the second Psalm says about Jesus: 'You are my Son. Today I have become your Father.'" Here is another example in Psalm 16:9–11. "No wonder my heart is glad, and I rejoice. My body rests in safety. For you will not leave my soul among the dead or allow your holy one to rot in the grave. You will show me the way of life, granting me the joy of your presence and the pleasures of living with you forever."

Then the Bible even describes that all nations will hear His holiness. We can attest to that because Christianity has survived throughout the ages. Here is what the Old Testament says in Isaiah 2:3: "People from many nations will come and say, 'Come, let us go up to the mountain of the Lord, to the house of Jacob's God. There he will teach us his ways, and we will walk in his paths.' For the Lord's teaching will go out from Zion; his word will go out from Jerusalem." Jesus's ministry initially stayed in the Jerusalem region (Judea, Samaria, Galilee), spreading out from there because of His disciples. John 4:25 says, "The woman said, 'I know the Messiah is coming—the one who is called Christ. When he comes, he will explain everything to us.'" It is essential to know that this woman was a Samaritan, a foreigner whom Jews of that time didn't get along with.

As the last example, Jesus was born of Mary, a virgin at the time of conception. That event was predicted in Isaiah 7:14. "All right then, the Lord Himself will give you the sign. Look! The virgin will conceive a child! She will give birth to a son and call Him Immanuel (God is with us)." The Gospels of Matthew and Luke confirm this detail. I make these points because it's impossible to write off these events as coincidences.

APPLICABLE TO MODERN LIFE

I have stated this before, but the Bible is still relevant even though it hasn't changed. Regardless of how old the text is, it is incredible to see advice, guidance, words of affirmation, and lessons that help us through our situations today. Some recorded fantastic accounts might seem impossible, but there is always something greater being said behind those stories. I am defending God's word; for example, see what is encouraged in Jude 1:3. "Dear friends, I had been eagerly planning to write to you about the salvation we all share. But now I find that I must write about something else, urging you to defend the faith that God has entrusted once for all time to his holy people." Here is another reason I write this book: "You have been believers so long now that you ought to be teaching others. Instead, you need someone to teach you again the basic things about God's word. You are like babies who need milk and cannot eat solid food" (Hebrews 5:12). I had been complacent for a long time by not fulfilling the Great Commission, which Jesus set. Why not utilize the gifts God has given me? I might not understand things perfectly, but I believe God wanted me to do this.

Given today's generation, 2 Peter 2:18–19 seems eerily similar to what is happening. "They brag about themselves with empty, foolish boasting. With an appeal to twisted sexual desires, they lure back into sin those who have barely escaped from a lifestyle of deception. They promise freedom, but they themselves are slaves of sin and corruption. For you are a slave to whatever controls you." Granted, I am not free from fault either. I have made mistakes like this and have been nearly convinced to go down a specific path by those who had significant influence.

I love the wisdom that scripture offers about pain and discipline. Pain and discipline are supposed to be character building. See Hebrews

12:11. "No discipline is enjoyable while it is happening—it's painful! But afterward there will be a peaceful harvest of right living for those who are trained in this way." It is neither my goal nor the original author's goal to cause pain. We have to risk the potential to cause pain when speaking the truth, but we don't appreciate it when it does. Second Corinthians 7:9 says, "Now I am glad I sent it, not because it hurt you, but because the pain caused you to repent and change your ways. It was the kind of sorrow God wants his people to have, so you were not harmed by us in any way." We can be glad that any pain causes people to change, but we don't have to be delighted that the experience was painful.

Speaking in flowery language isn't my intent either. Making a message confusing on purpose is an odd thing to do. I wanted to use logic and terminology that are accessible to anybody willing to listen. First Corinthians 14:9 says, "It's the same for you. If you speak to people in words they don't understand, how will they know what you are saying? You might as well be talking into empty space." What purpose is there in using language only likeminded people understand? There is a reason called "preaching to the choir." I pray that my words have been understandable.

The book of Proverbs has excellent godly wisdom that applies to everyday life. I highly suggest reading this whole book in the Bible. Here are some of my favorites:

1. Proverbs 18:13: "Spouting off before listening to the facts is both shameful and foolish."
2. Proverbs 17:15: "Acquitting the guilty and condemning the innocent—both are detestable to the Lord."
3. Proverbs 16:1, 3: "We can make our own plans, but the Lord gives the right answer. Commit your actions to the Lord, and your plans will succeed."

"FAIRY TALES" IN SCRIPTURE

The Bible contains stories about fantastic events that haven't been seen again. Just because an account has fantasy elements doesn't mean it isn't true. The Bible talks about the world being spoken into existence and mentions a talking serpent, a talking donkey, a great tower built into the heavens and God cursing men through confusing the languages, a man being swallowed by a great fish, fire from heaven, and more. I refer to a quote from Shakespeare's *Hamlet*: "There are more things in heaven and earth than are dreamt of in human philosophy." While they may be uncommon, there are a lot of unexplained events in modern history that defy scientific explanations. We have discovered new things about our current world and the expanse we call "space" that seem to defy our understanding of physics. The original authors of those stories in scripture have no motive to lie, especially when manuscripts record these events. How can we attest to delusion if we weren't there to observe these events? It is impossible to make that assumption. Theoretically, anything is possible, but that is the thing: it is purely theoretical. Not only that, but it is a theory that is impossible to test. It isn't a good theory if you have to make presuppositions such as "It must have been a delusion because those things couldn't have happened because they are too fantastical to be real."

How do we explain moments when doctors are astonished at someone's survival when there are no chances? How can we define our consciousness? It is especially curious when studies of near-death experiences record people who were still aware of their surroundings. How can we explain the beauty of creation? How do we explain the micromachines necessary for life? How do we define a genetic code built from specific proteins to make those machines work? How do we explain thousands of manuscripts that, when written, described events that had yet to take place in history?

QUESTION 14: HOW DO WE KNOW RANDOM PEOPLE DIDN'T CONSPIRE TO CREATE THE BIBLE?

In this chapter, I address a conspiracy theory some believe about Christianity. Many have said that the Catholic Church changed what was written to exercise power. Others say groups of people conspired to make up the content found in scripture. In the first place, how would anyone have the mind to make up the content found in the Bible? The Catholic Church would have to have edited thousands of manuscripts to accomplish that task. There would have to have been ingenious storytellers to develop the tens of thousands of verses that all tie together. It would have taken hundreds of people to make up names, numbers, events, life stories, poetry, history, and prophecy. In a sense, this claim is comparable to the ludicrous conspiracy theory of a flat earth. I argue, "What purpose would the group of people have to supposedly lie by writing about the love and joy found in scripture?" Hundreds, if not thousands, of people died while telling the scripture story and didn't socially benefit from telling a supposed lie. The issue is often with people who used or use scripture as an excuse to accomplish vile deeds. Our mission isn't conquest, and it should never have been used as an excuse for atrocities committed.

Here is a brutal truth: people aren't perfect, even Christians. There were many bad actors in the Christian faith after Jesus's time. I cannot condone the corruption, torture, and murder old "Christians" committed in His name. Those acts weren't right and should never have been condoned. It is unspeakably corrupt to commit evil and claim it is done for a righteous purpose. People have used the Word of God to establish authoritarian rule. God doesn't want us to be tyrants. He wants us to love Him and people. Those are the two great commandments. First Timothy 6:4–5 is a pretty good representation of what I'm saying here. "Anyone who teaches something different is arrogant and lacks understanding. Such a person has an unhealthy desire to quibble over the meaning of words. This stirs up arguments ending in jealousy, division, slander, and evil suspicions. These people always cause trouble. Their minds are corrupt, and they have turned their backs on the truth. To them, a show of godliness is just a way to become wealthy." I have to be cautious in what I say in this book because I have argued over the meaning of words (basically over nothing). Some church denominations still argue over this issue, and it has caused division. I understand why skeptics accuse us of wanting power and money. We argue over stupid things and often become greedy.

FACT-BASED PLAN

The examples I've provided show that the Bible is historical, detailed, prophetic, rational, and applicable. God knows we are limited in knowledge and desire more because of the initial sin. Sometimes that desire overtakes us and makes us focus on details that don't matter. However, this can also be the best evidence for God. God also knew this would happen; He knew we would be susceptible to doubt. I propose this is why God wanted to use prophecy, history, and detail in His Word. He wants us to lean on His Word instead of other people's understanding. I write this book only to point you to His Word and provide some of my knowledge, because I believe it is required based on what He says. Please don't depend on my understanding either. I highly encourage you to read the Good Book yourself with the intent to study and understand it.

5

THE ULTIMATE
PURPOSE

I have been building up to my final point by giving examples of smaller strategies I see in the Bible. There is a scripture-wide strategy I must include for the sake of spreading the good news. First, let's dive into the wonder of creation as a form of expressing His creativity. Psalm 19:1–4 says, "The heavens proclaim the glory of God. The skies display his craftsmanship. Day after day they continue to speak; night after night they make him known. They speak without a sound or word; their voice is never heard. Yet their message has gone throughout the earth, and their words to all the world. God has made a home in the heavens for the sun." Scientists can see what wonders of the galaxy there are today. There are beautiful nebulas, awe-inspiring celestial clouds, cataclysmic solar explosions, devastating black holes, matter that is invisible to the naked eye, and intricate dances of gravitational pull.

Look at what is around us on earth as well. There are millions of species of all sorts of animals with their societal behaviors, unknown counts of cellular life forms with unique DNA, exquisite nanomachines that make life possible, and plant species that produce the oxygen we breathe and consume the carbon dioxide we output. There are also cycles of weather necessary to sustain the planet, internal metallurgical movement that creates a gigantic magnetic field to protect us from solar flares, and people who can communicate and rationally relate to one another. I could go on and on by listing miraculous qualities of our lives.

QUESTION 15: THE WORLD IS MEANINGLESS. WHY BOTHER? WHAT IS THE POINT?

How can the world and the universe we live in be meaningless? How can a random mechanism produce beauty when there is supposedly no reason for such beauty? It is far more logical and meaningful if there is a designer for the designs we observe. I can hardly imagine the visual of creation given the detail provided in scripture. How wonderful that must have looked! I long for more information hidden from us, since my mind desires creativity. How deep is the knowledge of God? He knew that the universe required very particular circumstances for life to be necessary. He knew our bodies needed intricate cellular mechanisms to function. He knew we would argue about all sorts of problems in the world because He made us rational. He knew we would all decide to follow our path and needed saving. He knew that the law wouldn't be enough for His people. Everything in scripture points to something greater.

It was impossible from the start for people to earn their way to salvation. God's law was used to show how difficult it was and is to be holy. Acts 13:38–39 says, "Brothers, listen! We are here to proclaim that through this man Jesus there is forgiveness for your sins. Everyone who believes in him is made right in God's sight—something the law of Moses could never do." We know this is the truth because every time the Hebrew people sinned, a sacrifice was required to cleanse that sin. This was a never-ending cycle that could never clean someone completely. The not-so-secret secret hinted at in Hebrews 11 shows that the righteous in the Old Testament never depended solely on the law. The law was important, but they all followed it to their best ability due to their faith in God. They accomplished everything recorded through their trust in Him. God has permanently changed lives for the better. Many lost and broken people from evil societies changed their minds and focused on God. Rahab changed her mind about God, was adopted by the Hebrews, and became part of the lineage of Jesus because she recognized that what she had been doing was wrong. Some of the Ninevites set for destruction turned toward God because of Jonah. God found favor among many people while they committed evil acts because they recognized their sin and turned from it. Is this not the same message Jesus taught? Hadn't their lives been transformed drastically?

God uses imperfect people to fulfill His great plan and changes them to do good for His purpose. David did a lot of horrible things throughout his life. He committed adultery, murdered a man because of that, and directly disobeyed God by starting temple construction early. Yet God forgave him because David recognized he had sinned. David always turned back. Repentance is why God wanted Jesus to be from David's lineage. David was humble enough to admit his mistakes even when he was a great king! Moses initially made many excuses to God about his ability to speak, but he later became known for being a strong leader. Moses learned to trust God. He made a mistake by striking the rock when God told him not to and suffered by not entering the Promised Land, but he was still faithful enough to instruct the next leader to fulfill God's promise. Israel had turned their backs on God over and over. They always managed to come back to God. God established rulers in their lives that brought them back to His ways. God always redeemed those who admitted their mistakes. Jesus offers that same redemption if we are willing to believe He died for our sins. Recognizing a problem in your life comes first. Knowing that you can never do enough to save yourself is essential.

Life will be challenging if we accept this gift of grace. Our safety cannot be guaranteed on this earth due to the curse. We all wish it would be different, and it will be. There will be times when you experience hardship. Ask God to give you the strength to endure it. Accept people's love, compassion, and care because God had prompted them to offer it. God may speak to you in ways you don't expect. Be diligent in praying as often as you can. Some do this daily, some do it more often, and some rarely do it. I can attest that it helps immensely to do it more often than not. Learn to give people grace if they aren't behaving correctly in your time of need. Also, be bold enough to tell them how you want to be treated. I have often been guilty of trying to counsel before listening when people are hurting. My behavior was foolish since they weren't expecting counsel. In our speech, Jesus teaches us to be compassionate, kind, and merciful.

If you are starting your journey, asking questions is entirely valid and encouraged. It is imperative to seek counsel if you need help understanding something. Be willing to trust someone you know who is an excellent example of a Christian to help you. Try going to church and see if you can learn something about the culture and preaching style of the pastor. Make sure to let people know if they are being too harsh in their words. Call us out on our hypocrisy. Everyone is guilty of something; don't let anybody fool you. Read the Bible in whatever version makes the most sense to you at first. God won't fault us for trying to understand His Word in the best way we can. If you must, you could even look into a good audio Bible if you prefer that. I encourage you to take notes and highlight things you want to understand better.

Suppose you feel that an inner voice is speaking to you about any conviction you might have; listen and figure out why you might feel wrong. The beginning steps are simple if you conclude that there is something to what we say. Confess that you have done wrong in your life. I am not accusing you through this declaration. The Bible tells us that we are all sinners. The conviction must come from your thoughts. Persecution isn't the Christian way. A genuine Christian will say to you that everyone sins and might give examples of sins that exist without throwing specific accusations against particular people. Sin is the act of wanting to do things your way without God's help.

After acknowledging you are guilty through admission, you must then believe that Jesus died on the cross for our sins. Jesus is the perfect sacrifice who could cover the tremendous cost of sin. I cannot deny He exists because the record shows He did, and His disciples certainly didn't die for no reason. Who would be willing to die for a lie that caused such suffering and persecution? Many disciples ended up poor, in jail, and executed for their faith. Your journey won't be perfect. Paul struggled with his sin while having faith in Jesus. Many church people and disciples had terrible habits they had to grow out of. They always confessed that they were guilty and then asked for forgiveness. Repentance is a deep regret about your actions and a turning to God for help. Once you make an effort to change for the better by praying, doing what is right, and sustaining your belief, the process eventually becomes a little easier because you keep trusting God to help with what you cannot do by yourself.

Keep on reading the Bible. One of my favorite acronyms is BIBLE: Basic Instructions Before Leaving Earth. Establish friendships with Christians who will build your faith. These are vital. The last instruction is probably the hardest. When the Holy Spirit leads you to be confident, you should be able to share the same gospel found in scripture with other people. Jesus commands His disciples to spread the good news and make disciples of all nations. God will lead you to do what you must if you listen to His Holy Spirit.

I pray for those who haven't decided. Choosing to believe is the most important thing a person will ever do because his or her spiritual, eternal life is at stake. Anyone who doesn't believe that Jesus came down as God in the form of a man who died for our sins will experience eternal separation from God. The Bible says there is weeping and gnashing of teeth in the place described as the lake of fire in the book of Revelation. I sincerely wish all would come to know God just like He desires. The reality is truly heartbreaking because many won't ultimately accept Him for who He is: the Greatest Strategist, who planned everything ahead of time so they might be convinced He loves them through His Son.

VERSE APPENDIX

This section provides a quick reference of verses mentioned in the book that aren't directly quoted. Some sections mention whole chapters of the Bible. For the sake of brevity, I will refer to chapters to encourage you to read them yourself. All verses are from the New Living Translation since that version is the easiest to understand while preserving the original context, in my opinion.

CHAPTER 1

- Proverbs 3:5: "Trust in the Lord with all your heart; do not depend on your own understanding."
- Romans 12:2: "Don't copy the behavior and customs of this world, but let God transform you into a new person by changing the way you think. Then you will learn to know God's will for you, which is good and pleasing and perfect."
- James 3:12–18: "Does a fig tree produce olives, or a grapevine produce figs? No, and you can't draw fresh water from a salty spring. If you are wise and understand God's ways, prove it by living an honorable life, doing good works with the humility that comes from wisdom. But if you are bitterly jealous and there is selfish ambition in your heart, don't cover up the truth with boasting and lying. For jealousy and selfishness are not God's kind of wisdom. Such things are earthly, unspiritual, and demonic. For wherever there is jealousy and selfish ambition, there you will find disorder and evil of every kind. But the wisdom from above is first of all pure. It is also peace loving, gentle at all times, and willing to yield to others. It is full of mercy and the fruit of good

deeds. It shows no favoritism and is always sincere. And those who are peacemakers will plant seeds of peace and reap a harvest of righteousness."

- 1 Corinthians 3:18–20: "Stop deceiving yourselves. If you think you are wise by this world's standards, you need to become a fool to be truly wise. For the wisdom of this world is foolishness to God. As the Scriptures say, 'He traps the wise in the snare of their own cleverness.' And again, 'The Lord knows the thoughts of the wise; he knows they are worthless.'"

- Proverbs 3:7: "Don't be impressed with your own wisdom. Instead, fear the Lord and turn away from evil."

- Joshua 1:8: "Study this Book of Instruction continually. Meditate on it day and night so you will be sure to obey everything written in it. Only then will you prosper and succeed in all you do."

- Genesis 12:2–3: "I will make you into a great nation. I will bless you and make you famous, and you will be a blessing to others. I will bless those who bless you and curse those who treat you with contempt. All the families on earth will be blessed through you."

- Genesis 17:4–8: "This is my covenant with you: I will make you the father of a multitude of nations! What's more, I am changing your name. It will no longer be Abram. Instead, you will be called Abraham, for you will be the father of many nations. I will make you extremely fruitful. Your descendants will become many nations, and kings will be among them! I will confirm my covenant with you and your descendants after you, from generation to generation. This is the everlasting covenant: I will always be your God and the God of your descendants after you. And I will give the entire land of Canaan, where you now live as a foreigner, to you and your descendants. It will be their possession forever, and I will be their God."

- Exodus 2:24–25: "God heard their groaning, and he remembered his covenant promise to Abraham, Isaac, and Jacob. He looked down on the people of Israel and knew it was time to act."

- Exodus 3:8: "So I have come down to rescue them from the power of the Egyptians and lead them out of Egypt into their own fertile and spacious land. It is a land flowing with milk and honey—the land where the Canaanites, Hittites, Amorites, Perizzites, Hivites, and Jebusites now live."

CHAPTER 2

- 1 John 1:8–10: "If we claim we have no sin, we are only fooling ourselves and not living in the truth. But if we confess our sins to Him, he is faithful and just to forgive us our sins and to cleanse us from all wickedness. If we claim we have not sinned, we are calling God a liar and showing that his word has no place in our hearts."
- Genesis 19:4–9: "But before they retired for the night, all the men of Sodom, young and old, came from all over the city and surrounded the house. They shouted to Lot, 'Where are the men who came to spend the night with you? Bring them out to us so we can have sex with them!' So Lot stepped outside to talk to them, shutting the door behind him. 'Please, my brothers,' he begged, 'don't do such a wicked thing. Look, I have two virgin daughters. Let me bring them out to you, and you can do with them as you wish. But please, leave these men alone, for they are my guests and are under my protection.' 'Stand back!' they shouted. 'This fellow came to town as an outsider, and now he's acting like our judge! We'll treat you far worse than those other men!' And they lunged toward Lot to break down the door."
- Numbers 14:13–16: "But Moses objected. 'What will the Egyptians think when they hear about it?' he asked the Lord. 'They know full well the power you displayed in rescuing your people from Egypt. Now if you destroy them, the Egyptians will send a report to the inhabitants of this land, who have already heard that you live among your people. They know, Lord, that you have appeared to your people face to face and that your pillar of cloud hovers over them. They know that you go before them in the pillar of cloud by day and pillar of fire by night. Now if you slaughter all these people with a single blow the nations that have heard of your fame will say, "The Lord was not able to bring them into the land he swore to give them, so he killed them in the wilderness."'"

- Genesis 3:19: "By the sweat of your brow will you have food to eat until you return to the ground from which you were made. For you were made from dust, and to dust you will return."
- Genesis 3:22–23: "Then the Lord God said, 'Look, the human beings have become like us, knowing both good and evil. What if they reach out, take fruit from the tree of life, and eat it? Then they will live forever!' So the Lord God banished them from the Garden of Eden, and sent Adam out to cultivate the ground from which he had been made."
- Romans 6:23: "For the wages of sin is death, but the free gift of God is eternal life through Christ Jesus our Lord."
- Psalm 5:4: "O God, you take no pleasure in wickedness; you cannot tolerate the sins of the wicked."
- Isaiah 55:8–9: "'My thoughts are nothing like your thoughts,' says the Lord. 'And my ways are far beyond anything you could imagine. For just as the heavens are higher than the earth, so my ways are higher than your ways and my thoughts higher than your thoughts.'"
- 2 Samuel 12:19–21: "When David saw them whispering, he realized what had happened. 'Is the child dead?' He asked. 'Yes,' they replied, 'he is dead.' Then David got up from the ground, washed himself, put on lotions, and changed his clothes. He went to the Tabernacle and worshiped the Lord. After that, he returned to the palace and was served food and ate. His advisers were amazed. 'We don't understand you,' they told him. 'While the child was still living, you wept and refused to eat. But now that the child is dead, you have stopped your mourning and are eating again.'"
- Judges 7:12: "The armies of Midian, Amalek, and the people of the east had settled in the valley like a swarm of locusts. Their camels were like grains of sand on the seashore–too many to count!"
- Isaiah 48:8: "Yes, I will tell you of things that are entirely new, things you never heard of before. For I know so well what traitors you are. You have been rebels from birth."
- Isaiah 48:10–11: "I have refined you, but not as silver is refined. Rather, I have refined you in the furnace of suffering. I will rescue

you for my sake —yes, for my own sake! I will not let my reputation be tarnished, and I will not share my glory with idols!'"

- Matthew 7:1–2: "Do not judge others, and you will not be judged. For you will be treated as you treat others. The standards you use in judging is the standard by which you will be judged."

CHAPTER 3

- Joshua 2:1–14: "Then Joshua secretly sent out two spies from the Israelite camp at Acacia Grove. He instructed them, 'Scout out the land on the other side of the Jordan River, especially around Jericho.' So the two men set out and came to the house of a prostitute named Rahab and stayed there that night. But someone told the king of Jericho, 'Some Israelites have come here tonight to spy out the land.' So the king of Jericho sent orders to Rahab: 'Bring out the men who have come into your house, for they have come here to spy out the whole land.' Rahab had hidden the two men, but she replied, 'Yes, the men were here earlier, but I didn't know where they were from. They left the town at dusk, as the gates were about to close. I don't know where they went. If you hurry, you can probably catch up with them.' (Actually, she had taken them up to the roof and hidden them beneath bundles of flax she had laid out.) So the king's men had left, the gate of Jericho was shut. Before the spies went to sleep that night, Rahab went up on the roof to talk with them. 'I know the Lord has given you this land, she told them. 'We are all afraid of you. Everyone in the land is living in terror. For we have heard how the Lord made a dry path for you through the Red Sea when you left Egypt. And we know what you did to Sihon and Og, the two Amorite kings east of the Jordan River, whose people you completely destroyed. No wonder our hearts have melted in fear! No one has the courage to fight after hearing such things. For the Lord your God is the supreme God of the heavens above and the earth below. Now swear to me by the Lord that you will be kind to me and my family since I have helped you. Give me some guarantee that. When Jericho is conquered, you will let me live, along with my father and mother, my brothers and sisters, and all their families. We offer our own lives as a guarantee for your safety,' the men agreed. 'If you don't betray us, we will keep our promise and be kind to you when the Lord gives us the land.'"

- Esther 5:4: "And Esther replied, 'If it pleases the king, let the king and Haman come today to a banquet I have prepared for the king.'"
- Esther 7:3: "Queen Esther replied, 'If I found favor with the king, and if it pleases the king to grant my request, I ask that my life and the lives of my people will be spared.'"
- Esther 8:5: "Esther said, 'If it pleases the king, and if I have found favor with him, and if he thinks it is right, and if I am pleasing to him, let there be a decree that reverses the orders of Haman son of Hammedatha the Agagite, who ordered the Jews throughout all the king's provinces should be destroyed.'"
- Esther 9:13: "Esther responded, 'If it pleases the king, give the Jews in Susa permission to do again tomorrow as they have done today, and let the bodies of Haman's ten sons be impaled on a pole.'"
- Genesis 34:5: "Soon Jacob heard that Shechem had defiled his daughter, Dinah. But since his sons were out in the fields herding his livestock, he said nothing until they returned."
- Genesis 34:7: "Meanwhile, Jacob's sons had come in from the field as soon as they heard what had happened. They were shocked and furious that their sister had been raped. Shechem had done a disgraceful thing against Jacob's family, something that should never be done."
- Genesis 34:25–27: "But three days later, when their wounds were still sore, two of Jacob's sons, Simenon and Levi, who were Dinah's full brothers, took their swords and entered the town without opposition. Then they slaughtered every male there. Including Hamor and his son Shechem. They killed them with their swords, then they took Dinah from Shechem's house and returned to their camp. Meanwhile, the rest of Jacob's sons arrived. Finding the men slaughtered, they plundered the town because their sister had been defiled there."

- Genesis 34:31: "'But why should we let him treat our sister like a prostitute?' They retorted angrily."
- Judges 20:4–6: "The Levite, the husband of the woman who had been murdered, said, 'My concubine and I came to spend the night in Gibran, a town that belongs to the people of Benjamin. That night some of the leading citizens of Gibran surrounded the house, planning to kill me, and they raped my concubine until she was dead. So I cut her body into twelve pieces and sent the pieces throughout the territory assigned to Israel, for these men have committed a terrible and shameful crime.'"
- Judges 20:12–13: "The Israelites sent messengers to the tribe of Benjamin, saying, 'What a terrible thing has been done among you! Give up those evil men, those troublemakers from Gibran, so we can execute them and purge Israel of this evil.'"
- Judges 20:35: "So the Lord helped Israel defeat Benjamin, and that day the Israelites killed 25,100 of Benjamin's warriors, all of whom were experienced swordsmen."
- 2 Samuel 13:14: "But Amnon wouldn't listen to her, and since he was stronger than she was, he raped her."
- 2 Samuel 13:16: "'No, no!' Tamar cried. 'Sending me away now is worse than what you've already done to me.'"
- 2 Samuel 13:19–22: "But now Tamar tore her robe and put ashes on her head. And then, with her face in her hands, she went away crying. Her brother Absalom saw her and asked, 'Is it true that Amnon has been with you? Well, my sister, keep quiet for now, since he's your brother. Don't worry about it.' So Tamar lived as a desolate woman in her brother Absalom's house. When King David heard what happened, he was very angry. And though Absalom never spoke to Amnon about this, he hated Amnon deeply because of what he had done to his sister."
- 2 Samuel 13:28–29: "Absalom told his men, 'Wait until Amnon gets drunk; then at my signal, kill him! Don't be afraid. I'm the one who has given the command. Take courage and do it!' So at Absalom's signal they murdered Amnon. Then the other sons of the king jumped on their mules and fled."

- Romans 1:26–27: "That is why God abandoned them to their shameful desires. Even the women turned against the natural way to have sex and instead indulged in sex with each other. And the men, instead of having normal sexual relations with women, burned with lust for each other. Men did shameful things with other men, and as a result of this sin, they suffered within themselves the penalty they deserved."

- 1 Corinthians 6:9: "Don't you realize that those who do wrong will not inherit the Kingdom of God? Don't fool yourselves. Those who indulge in sexual sin, or who worship idols, or commit adultery, or are male prostitutes, or practice homosexuality."

- 1 Timothy 1:10–11: "The law is for people who are sexually immoral, or who practice homosexuality, or are slave traders, liars, promise breakers, or who do anything else that contradicts the wholesome teaching. That comes from the glorious Good News entrusted to me by your blessed God."

ACKNOWLEDGMENTS

First and foremost, I dedicate this book to my personal Savior, Jesus Christ. His Holy Spirit guided me to become bold and courageous after spending most of my life being lukewarm. He is the only inspiration that truly matters. This book wouldn't be possible without the encouragement from one of my pastors at Epiphany Station. Pastor Pete Lee helped me hash out the difficult wording along with checking my work to be consistent with what God's word teaches.

Several authors I love made me realize I needed to change my life and dedicate my time to serving God. These authors include John Burke, Jordan Peterson, C. S. Lewis, Randy Alcorn, Lee Strobel, Nabeel Qureshi, Gregory Koukl, Kevin DeYoung, and more. Reading books by these authors helped me grow in faith and be inspired to take special care and time to study the scriptures intently. There are great mysteries found within those pages; do not miss the great opportunity of knowing who God is through his word. My final request for any Christian is to pass this book along to someone who has struggled with these questions. Be a good example and show some love to those who are lost. God bless you.

Printed in the United States
by Baker & Taylor Publisher Services